AUTISM
Introduction to a Neurodiverse World

Gareth Croot

Published by Divergent Consultants

For my Children Cleo-Emma and Nyle
In understanding your challenges you have made me face up to my own

And to my amazing wife Lindy
Thank you for your patience – I know in our little neurodiverse family I
am the most difficult.

<u>Chapter 1: Understanding Autism Spectrum Disorder (ASD)</u>

Autism Spectrum Disorder (ASD) is a developmental disorder that affects communication, social interaction, and behavior. It is a spectrum disorder, which means that it affects individuals differently and to varying degrees. Some individuals with ASD may have mild symptoms, while others may have severe impairments that impact their ability to function in daily life. In this chapter, we will explore what ASD is, its characteristics, prevalence, and demographics, and the history of its diagnosis and research in the UK.

ASD Characteristics

The main characteristics of ASD include challenges in social interaction, communication, and behavior. Individuals with ASD may have difficulty understanding social cues, making eye contact, or engaging in conversation. They may have trouble with nonverbal communication, such as facial expressions or body language. They may also exhibit repetitive behaviors or interests, have sensory sensitivities, or display difficulty with transitions and changes in routine.

ASD Prevalence and Demographics in the UK

In the UK, approximately 1 in 100 people have ASD, according to the National Autistic Society. It affects individuals of all races, ethnicities, and socioeconomic backgrounds. However, research has shown that children from disadvantaged backgrounds are more likely to have undiagnosed ASD. The prevalence of ASD has increased in recent years, which some experts attribute to improved diagnosis and awareness.

ASD Diagnosis and Research in the UK
The history of ASD diagnosis and research in the UK dates back to the early 20th century when doctors first recognized it as a distinct disorder. In the 1940s, child psychiatrist Leo Kanner published a paper describing a group of children who displayed a pattern of behaviors that he called "early infantile autism." Kanner's work laid the foundation for the modern understanding of ASD.

In the following decades, researchers began to refine the diagnostic criteria for ASD, leading to the inclusion of Asperger's syndrome and pervasive developmental disorder not otherwise specified (PDD-NOS) as part of the spectrum. In the UK, the National Institute for Health and Care Excellence (NICE) provides guidance on the diagnosis and management of ASD.

Research on ASD in the UK has led to a better understanding of its causes and potential treatments. Studies have identified genetic mutations and environmental factors that may contribute to the development of ASD, including prenatal exposure to certain toxins or infections. Additionally, research has shown that early intervention and behavioural therapy can improve outcomes for individuals with ASD.

Chapter 2: Neurodiversity and the Autism Spectrum

Neurodiversity is a concept that refers to the diversity of human brains and the different ways they function. It recognizes that neurological differences are natural and should be celebrated rather than pathologized. Autism Spectrum Disorder (ASD) is a condition that is commonly associated with neurodiversity. In this chapter, we will explore what neurodiversity is, how it applies to ASD, the different perspectives on neurodiversity and ASD, and the benefits and challenges of embracing neurodiversity in society.

Understanding Neurodiversity and How it Applies to ASD
Neurodiversity is an approach to understanding the human mind that acknowledges that differences in brain function are natural and not necessarily disorders. It recognizes that people with different neurological profiles can have unique strengths, weaknesses, and perspectives. ASD is a condition that is commonly associated with neurodiversity because it is a neurological difference that affects the way people process information and interact with the world around them.

Exploring the Different Perspectives on Neurodiversity and ASD
There are different perspectives on the relationship between neurodiversity and ASD. Some people view ASD as a medical condition that needs to be cured or treated. They may focus on the negative aspects of ASD, such as the challenges it can present in social interaction and communication. Others view ASD as a natural variation in human cognition and advocate for accepting and celebrating neurodiversity. They may emphasize the strengths of ASD, such as attention to detail and a unique perspective on the world.

Benefits and Challenges of Embracing Neurodiversity in Society

Embracing neurodiversity can have significant benefits for individuals with ASD and society as a whole. By recognizing the unique strengths and perspectives of individuals with ASD, we can create a more inclusive and accepting society. This can lead to increased opportunities for individuals with ASD to participate in society and contribute to their communities. Additionally, recognizing the strengths of individuals with ASD can lead to greater innovation and creativity in fields such as science, technology, and the arts.

However, embracing neurodiversity can also present challenges. Some people may struggle to understand or accept neurodivergent behaviors and perspectives, which can lead to discrimination and marginalization. Additionally, some individuals with ASD may face barriers to accessing education, employment, and healthcare. Addressing these challenges requires a commitment to promoting education and awareness about neurodiversity and ensuring that individuals with ASD have access to the resources and support they need to succeed.

UK Initiatives on Embracing Neurodiversity
The UK has made significant strides in recent years to promote neurodiversity and support individuals with ASD. The UK government has recognized the importance of embracing neurodiversity and has implemented policies to promote inclusion and accessibility. For example, the Autism Act 2009 mandates that the government develop a national autism strategy and improve access to services for individuals with ASD.

Additionally, the UK has several organizations and initiatives that promote neurodiversity and support individuals with ASD. The National Autistic Society provides resources and support for individuals with ASD and their families, while the Autism Research Trust funds research on the causes and potential treatments for ASD. The UK also has several neurodiverse-led organizations, such as Autistic UK and the Neurodiversity Movement, that advocate for the rights and inclusion of individuals with ASD and other neurological differences.

Overall, understanding and embracing neurodiversity can lead to a more inclusive and accepting society that recognizes and celebrates the unique strengths and perspectives of all individuals, including those with ASD. It is important for individuals, organizations, and governments to continue promoting awareness, education, and support for neurodiversity in the UK and around the world. By doing so, we can create a world that truly values and celebrates the diversity of human minds.

Chapter 3: Early Signs and Symptoms of ASD

Autism Spectrum Disorder (ASD) is a neurodevelopmental condition that affects communication, social interaction, and behavior. It is typically diagnosed in early childhood, and early intervention is essential for improving outcomes. In this chapter, we will explore the early signs and symptoms of ASD in infants and toddlers, the diagnostic process for ASD, and the importance of early intervention.

Identifying the Signs and Symptoms of ASD in Infants and Toddlers
The signs and symptoms of ASD can vary widely, and they may not be immediately apparent in infants and toddlers. However, there are some early signs that parents and caregivers can look out for. For example, infants with ASD may not respond to their name or engage in eye contact, may not smile in response to social cues, and may not engage in social play. Toddlers with ASD may struggle to make friends, may have difficulty with imaginative play, and may engage in repetitive behaviors such as lining up toys or flapping their hands.

It is important to note that not all children with ASD will exhibit these signs, and some children without ASD may exhibit some of these behaviors. However, if parents or caregivers are concerned about their child's development, they should talk to their paediatrician or a specialist in neurodevelopmental disorders.

Examining the Diagnostic Process for ASD
The diagnostic process for ASD typically involves a comprehensive evaluation by a team of specialists, including a paediatrician, a child psychologist or psychiatrist, and a speech and language therapist. The evaluation may include observation of the child's behavior and interactions, developmental assessments, and communication assessments.

In the UK, the National Institute for Health and Care Excellence (NICE) has established guidelines for the diagnosis and management of ASD. These guidelines recommend that ASD should be diagnosed by a specialist multidisciplinary team and that the diagnosis should be based on a comprehensive assessment of the child's developmental history, behavior, and communication.

Highlighting the Importance of Early Intervention
Early intervention is essential for improving outcomes for children with ASD. Research has shown that early intervention can lead to significant improvements in communication, social skills, and behavior. It can also improve outcomes in other areas such as academic achievement and independence.

In the UK, there are a range of early intervention services available for children with ASD and their families. These may include speech and language therapy, occupational therapy, and behavioural interventions. Early intervention services may be provided by the National Health Service (NHS), local authorities, or private providers.

It is important for parents and caregivers to seek early intervention services as soon as possible if they have concerns about their child's development. Early intervention can help children with ASD to develop the skills they need to communicate, interact with others, and succeed in school and life.

Chapter 4: Communication and Socialization in ASD

Autism Spectrum Disorder (ASD) is a developmental disorder that affects communication and socialization skills. Individuals with ASD may experience challenges in understanding and expressing verbal and non-verbal communication, making and maintaining social connections, and interpreting social cues. In this chapter, we will explore the communication and socialization challenges faced by individuals with ASD, the impact of these challenges on social and emotional development, and strategies for improving communication and socialization skills in individuals with ASD.

Exploring the Communication and Socialization Challenges Faced by Individuals with ASD
Individuals with ASD may experience challenges in a range of communication and socialization areas. These may include difficulty with:

Verbal and non-verbal communication: Individuals with ASD may struggle with using and understanding spoken language, facial expressions, body language, and tone of voice.

Social interaction: Individuals with ASD may struggle with making and maintaining friendships, engaging in reciprocal conversations, and understanding social norms and cues.

Empathy and emotional regulation: Individuals with ASD may struggle with identifying and regulating their own emotions and understanding the emotions of others.

These challenges can make it difficult for individuals with ASD to form meaningful social connections and navigate social situations.

Examining the Impact of These Challenges on Social and Emotional Development

The communication and socialization challenges faced by individuals with ASD can have a significant impact on social and emotional development. Without adequate support and intervention, individuals with ASD may be at risk of developing:

Social isolation: Difficulty with making and maintaining friendships may lead to social isolation and loneliness.

Anxiety and depression: Difficulty with interpreting and responding to social cues may lead to anxiety and depression.

Challenging behaviors: Difficulty with communicating wants and needs may lead to challenging behaviors such as tantrums and aggression.

It is important for parents, caregivers, and educators to understand the impact of these challenges on social and emotional development and to provide appropriate support and intervention.

Discussing Strategies for Improving Communication and Socialization Skills in Individuals with ASD

There are a range of strategies and interventions that can be used to support individuals with ASD in improving communication and socialization skills. These may include:

Social skills training: Social skills training may involve teaching individuals with ASD social norms and cues, how to initiate and maintain conversations, and how to interpret and respond to social cues.

Communication supports: Communication supports may include visual aids such as picture schedules, social stories, and visual supports for academic tasks.

Peer mentoring: Peer mentoring may involve pairing individuals with ASD with neurotypical peers to facilitate social interaction and friendship building.

Occupational therapy: Occupational therapy may involve addressing sensory processing issues that may be impacting communication and socialization.

Speech and language therapy: Speech and language therapy may involve addressing specific communication challenges such as articulation, expressive language, and receptive language.

It is important for parents, caregivers, and educators to work together to identify the individual needs and preferences of individuals with ASD and to provide appropriate support and intervention.

<u>**Chapter 5: Sensory Processing Differences in ASD**</u>

Sensory processing refers to the way our brains receive, interpret, and respond to sensory information from our environment. For individuals with Autism Spectrum Disorder (ASD), sensory processing differences can be a significant challenge. In this chapter, we will explore the sensory processing differences experienced by individuals with ASD, the impact of these differences on behavior and learning, and strategies for addressing sensory processing challenges in individuals with ASD.

Understanding the Sensory Processing Differences Experienced by Individuals with ASD
Individuals with ASD may experience differences in the way they process sensory information. These differences can include:

Hypersensitivity: Some individuals with ASD may be hypersensitive to sensory input, meaning that they experience sensory information as overwhelming or even painful. This can include sensitivity to bright lights, loud sounds, strong smells, and certain textures.

Hyposensitivity: Other individuals with ASD may be hyposensitive to sensory input, meaning that they do not experience sensory information as strongly as others. This can include a lack of awareness of pain or temperature, or a need for excessive sensory input such as touching or squeezing objects.

Difficulty with sensory integration: Some individuals with ASD may struggle to integrate sensory information from different senses. This can make it difficult to filter out irrelevant information and focus on what is important.

Examining the Impact of These Differences on Behavior and Learning

Sensory processing differences can have a significant impact on behavior and learning for individuals with ASD. Without adequate support and intervention, individuals with ASD may be at risk of developing:

Anxiety and stress: Sensory overload can cause anxiety and stress for individuals with ASD, leading to behavioural challenges such as tantrums and meltdowns.

Difficulty with social interaction: Sensory processing differences can impact social interaction by making it difficult to focus on conversation and interpret social cues.

Difficulty with academic tasks: Sensory processing differences can also impact academic tasks such as reading, writing, and listening.

It is important for parents, caregivers, and educators to understand the impact of sensory processing differences on behavior and learning and to provide appropriate support and intervention.

Discussing Strategies for Addressing Sensory Processing Challenges in Individuals with ASD

There are a range of strategies and interventions that can be used to support individuals with ASD in addressing sensory processing challenges. These may include:

Sensory diets: Sensory diets are personalized plans that incorporate specific sensory activities to address the individual's sensory needs. This may include activities such as swinging, bouncing, or brushing the skin.

Environmental modifications: Environmental modifications such as using noise-cancelling headphones or dimming the lights can help to reduce sensory overload.

Sensory breaks: Sensory breaks provide individuals with ASD with a break from sensory input to allow them to regulate their sensory systems.

Visual supports: Visual supports such as picture schedules and visual timetables can help to provide predictability and structure, reducing anxiety and stress.

It is important for parents, caregivers, and educators to work together to identify the individual sensory processing needs and preferences of individuals with ASD and to provide appropriate support and intervention.

Chapter 6: Co-occurring Conditions in ASD

Autism Spectrum Disorder (ASD) is a complex neurodevelopmental condition that affects individuals in varying degrees. While ASD is known for its core symptoms, such as difficulties in social communication and repetitive behaviors, it is also associated with a range of co-occurring conditions. Co-occurring conditions are disorders that occur alongside ASD and can impact the individual's health, well-being, and quality of life. It is essential to understand the common co-occurring conditions in individuals with ASD and how they can be managed.

According to the National Autistic Society, approximately 70% of individuals with ASD experience co-occurring conditions. The most common conditions seen in individuals with ASD include anxiety, depression, Attention Deficit Hyperactivity Disorder (ADHD), Obsessive-Compulsive Disorder (OCD), and epilepsy. These conditions can manifest differently in individuals with ASD and can affect their behavior, learning, and overall functioning.

Anxiety is one of the most common co-occurring conditions in individuals with ASD. It can cause significant distress and impair the individual's ability to function in daily life. Children with ASD are at a higher risk of developing anxiety compared to typically developing children. Some common signs of anxiety in individuals with ASD include social withdrawal, excessive worrying, sleep disturbances, and repetitive behaviors.

Depression is another co-occurring condition that affects individuals with ASD. Depression is a mood disorder characterized by persistent feelings of sadness, hopelessness, and disinterest in activities that were once enjoyed. Depression in individuals with ASD can be challenging to recognize, as they may not express their feelings verbally. Some signs of depression in individuals with ASD include decreased interest in social activities, changes in appetite, and sleep disturbances.

ADHD is a neurodevelopmental disorder characterized by symptoms such as hyperactivity, impulsivity, and inattention. Children with ASD are at a higher risk of developing ADHD than typically developing children. The symptoms of ADHD can overlap with those of ASD, making it challenging to distinguish between the two conditions. Some strategies for managing ADHD in individuals with ASD include behavioural therapy, medication, and parental support.

OCD is a co-occurring condition in individuals with ASD that is characterized by obsessions and compulsions. Obsessions are intrusive thoughts, images, or impulses that are often distressing and difficult to control. Compulsions are repetitive behaviors or mental acts that individuals feel compelled to perform in response to obsessions. OCD can be challenging to recognize in individuals with ASD as their repetitive behaviors may overlap with those of OCD. Some strategies for managing OCD in individuals with ASD include cognitive-behavioural therapy and medication.

Epilepsy is a neurological condition that causes seizures. Individuals with ASD are at a higher risk of developing epilepsy compared to typically developing individuals. Seizures in individuals with ASD can present differently, and their effects can vary from mild to severe. Some strategies for managing epilepsy in individuals with ASD include medication and lifestyle modifications.

Managing co-occurring conditions in individuals with ASD requires a multidisciplinary approach. The approach involves working with professionals from different fields, such as psychiatrists, neurologists, speech therapists, and occupational therapists. The treatment of co-occurring conditions should be tailored to meet the individual's needs and preferences.

Behavioural therapies, such as cognitive-behavioural therapy, can be effective in managing anxiety, depression, and OCD in individuals with ASD. These therapies aim to teach individuals how to recognize and challenge their negative thoughts and behaviors. Medication can also be used to manage co-occurring conditions in individuals with ASD. However, medication should only be used after careful consideration of the risks and benefits.

Parental support is essential in managing co-occurring conditions in individuals with ASD. Parents can play an active role in monitoring their child's behavior and symptoms and another common co-occurring condition in individuals with ASD is obsessive-compulsive disorder (OCD). OCD is a mental health disorder characterized by recurring unwanted thoughts, images, or impulses (obsessions) and repetitive behaviors or mental acts (compulsions) that individuals feel driven to perform. Individuals with ASD and OCD may experience more severe and impairing symptoms compared to those without ASD.

In addition to anxiety and OCD, ADHD is another common co-occurring condition in individuals with ASD. ADHD is a neurodevelopmental disorder that affects an individual's ability to sustain attention and control their impulses. Some of the symptoms of ADHD, such as hyperactivity, impulsivity, and difficulty with executive functioning, may overlap with symptoms of ASD.

The presence of co-occurring conditions can complicate the diagnosis and treatment of ASD. It is essential to assess and treat co-occurring conditions as part of the overall management of ASD. Treatment may involve medication, behavioural therapy, or a combination of both.

Behavioural therapy, such as cognitive-behavioural therapy (CBT), can be effective in managing co-occurring conditions. CBT focuses on identifying and changing negative thought patterns and behaviors that contribute to anxiety, OCD, or other co-occurring conditions. It can also help individuals with ASD develop coping skills to manage stress and anxiety.

In some cases, medication may be necessary to manage co-occurring conditions. Medications commonly prescribed for anxiety and OCD include selective serotonin reuptake inhibitors (SSRIs), while stimulant medication, such as methylphenidate or amphetamine, is commonly prescribed for ADHD. However, medication should be used in conjunction with behavioural therapy and under the guidance of a healthcare professional.

Chapter 7: Autism and Gender

Autism Spectrum Disorder (ASD) and gender identity are two complex and multifaceted aspects of human experience. As such, it is not surprising that these two domains of human experience intersect in unique ways. This chapter will explore the intersection of autism and gender identity, highlight the unique challenges faced by individuals with ASD who are transgender or non-binary, and discuss strategies for supporting the needs of these individuals.

Autism and Gender Identity

Recent research has shown that individuals with ASD are more likely to be transgender or non-binary than the general population. In a study conducted by the National Institutes of Health, it was found that individuals with ASD are nearly seven times more likely to be gender diverse than the general population. Another study conducted by the University of Cambridge found that around 8% of individuals with ASD also identify as transgender or gender diverse.

There are several possible explanations for the high prevalence of gender diversity in individuals with ASD. One theory is that the social and communication difficulties experienced by individuals with ASD may make it more difficult for them to conform to traditional gender norms and expectations. Additionally, the heightened sensitivity to sensory experiences experienced by many individuals with ASD may also make them more attuned to their own bodily experiences and sensations, including their gender identity.

Unique Challenges Faced by Individuals with ASD who are Transgender or Non-Binary

Individuals with ASD who are also transgender or non-binary face unique challenges that can make it difficult for them to navigate the world around them. For example, they may struggle with sensory overload in gendered spaces such as public restrooms, where the sounds and smells may be overwhelming. They may also have difficulty understanding and navigating social norms and expectations around gender expression and communication.

Additionally, individuals with ASD who are transgender or non-binary may face discrimination and marginalization from both the neurotypical and LGBTQ+ communities. They may be misunderstood and stigmatized for their intersectional identities, leading to increased levels of social isolation and mental health difficulties.

Strategies for Supporting the Needs of Individuals with ASD who are Transgender or Non-Binary

In order to support the needs of individuals with ASD who are transgender or non-binary, it is important to adopt a holistic and intersectional approach to their care. This may involve providing specialized support and resources to help them navigate both their gender identity and their ASD.

One strategy is to provide gender-neutral and sensory-friendly spaces in public areas, such as restrooms and changing rooms, to help mitigate sensory overload and reduce anxiety. This can create a more inclusive environment that recognizes and accommodates the diverse needs of individuals with ASD who are transgender or non-binary.

Another strategy is to provide specialized mental health support that addresses both their gender identity and their ASD. This may involve cognitive-behavioural therapy (CBT) or other therapeutic approaches that focus on coping skills and self-care. This can help individuals with ASD who are transgender or non-binary develop a stronger sense of self and resilience, which can help them navigate the challenges they may face.

Finally, it is essential to foster a culture of acceptance and inclusion that recognizes and celebrates the diversity of human experience. This may involve promoting awareness and education about autism and gender diversity in schools, workplaces, and other public settings. It can also involve advocating for policies and practices that promote equity and inclusion for all individuals, regardless of their gender identity or neurodiversity.

While research into the intersection of autism and gender identity is still limited, studies have shown that individuals with ASD are more likely to identify as transgender or gender non-conforming than the general population. This raises important questions about the unique challenges that these individuals face, as well as the support and resources that are available to them.

One of the challenges faced by individuals with ASD who are transgender or non-binary is a lack of understanding and acceptance from others. They may experience discrimination or bullying, both within and outside of the autism community. This can lead to feelings of isolation, low self-esteem, and mental health issues such as depression and anxiety.

Another challenge is accessing appropriate healthcare and support. Many healthcare providers lack knowledge and training around the intersection of autism and gender, leading to misdiagnosis or a lack of appropriate care. This can make it difficult for individuals with ASD who are transgender or non-binary to access the hormone therapy, surgery, or counselling that they need.

Despite these challenges, there are strategies that can be used to support the needs of individuals with ASD who are transgender or non-binary. One of the most important is education and awareness-raising. This includes educating healthcare providers, educators, and members of the general public about the intersection of autism and gender, and the unique challenges faced by these individuals. It also involves creating safe and inclusive spaces where individuals with ASD who are transgender or non-binary can feel accepted and supported.

Another strategy is providing access to appropriate healthcare and support services. This includes training healthcare providers in the intersection of autism and gender, as well as providing access to counselling, hormone therapy, and surgery for those who need it. It also involves creating support groups and community spaces where individuals with ASD who are transgender or non-binary can connect with others who share their experiences.

In addition, it is important to address the social and emotional needs of individuals with ASD who are transgender or non-binary. This includes providing support for mental health issues such as anxiety and depression, as well as developing strategies to address bullying and discrimination. It also involves promoting self-acceptance and self-care, and creating a sense of community and belonging for these individuals.

Chapter 8: Autism and Culture

Autism Spectrum Disorder (ASD) is a neurodevelopmental condition that affects individuals from all cultures and backgrounds. However, the way that autism is viewed and understood can vary greatly depending on cultural beliefs and practices. In this chapter, we will explore the impact of culture on the diagnosis and treatment of ASD, as well as the cultural differences in the presentation of ASD symptoms. We will also discuss strategies for providing culturally sensitive care for individuals with ASD.

Culture can play a significant role in the diagnosis and treatment of ASD. In some cultures, the symptoms of autism may not be seen as problematic, or may even be seen as desirable. For example, in some cultures, repetitive behaviors may be seen as a sign of discipline and self-control, rather than a symptom of autism. As a result, these behaviors may not be reported to healthcare professionals, leading to a delayed or missed diagnosis.

Cultural beliefs can also affect the types of treatments that are considered acceptable for individuals with ASD. For example, some cultures may prefer traditional or alternative medicine over Western medicine. Additionally, some cultures may view behavioural interventions, such as Applied Behavior Analysis (ABA), as disrespectful or culturally inappropriate.

The presentation of ASD symptoms can also vary across cultures. For example, in some cultures, social interactions may be less important than academic achievement, and individuals with ASD may be viewed as gifted or talented in certain areas. As a result, the social and communication difficulties associated with ASD may not be as noticeable or may be overlooked.

To provide culturally sensitive care for individuals with ASD, it is important to consider the cultural context in which they live. Healthcare professionals should be aware of cultural beliefs and practices that may impact the diagnosis and treatment of ASD, and should work collaboratively with families and communities to develop treatment plans that are acceptable and effective.

One strategy for providing culturally sensitive care is to involve cultural brokers or interpreters in the diagnosis and treatment process. Cultural brokers are individuals who have knowledge of both the cultural and healthcare systems and can facilitate communication between healthcare providers and families. Interpreters can also be used to ensure that families understand the diagnosis and treatment recommendations.

Another strategy is to provide culturally appropriate resources and materials for families. This can include translated materials or materials that reflect the cultural beliefs and practices of the family. Additionally, healthcare providers can work with families to identify cultural practices that may support or hinder the treatment process and develop strategies to work within those practices.

It is also important for healthcare providers to be aware of their own cultural biases and beliefs. Providers should strive to provide care that is free from bias and discrimination and should work to understand and respect the cultural beliefs and practices of their patients and families.

<u>**Chapter 9: Educational Support for Individuals with ASD**</u>

Education is crucial for all individuals, including those with Autism Spectrum Disorder (ASD). Early and appropriate educational support can significantly improve an individual's quality of life, allowing them to reach their full potential. This chapter explores the importance of educational support for individuals with ASD in the UK, the different types of educational settings and programs available, and effective strategies for supporting learning and development.

Education for Individuals with ASD

The education of individuals with ASD in the UK is protected under the Equality Act 2010, which ensures that individuals with disabilities are not discriminated against and are provided with reasonable adjustments. Children with ASD are entitled to receive the same education opportunities as their non-disabled peers. However, they may require additional support to access the curriculum.

Early intervention is key in providing educational support for children with ASD. Early diagnosis and intervention allow for tailored support to be put in place to address the individual's needs. The support provided must be individualized and based on the individual's strengths and needs.

Types of Educational Settings and Programs

There are several types of educational settings and programs available for individuals with ASD in the UK. These include mainstream schools, specialist schools, and home education.

Mainstream Schools

Mainstream schools are schools that provide education for all children, including those with disabilities. In the UK, the government recommends that children with disabilities attend mainstream schools wherever possible. However, mainstream schools may not always be able to meet the needs of children with ASD, and some children may require specialist support.

Specialist Schools

Specialist schools are schools that provide education for children with disabilities, including ASD. These schools provide a range of specialist support, including individualized education plans, speech and language therapy, occupational therapy, and counselling. Specialist schools provide a tailored curriculum that meets the individual needs of the children.

Home Education

Home education is another option available to parents of children with ASD in the UK. This option is suitable for children who may find it difficult to attend mainstream or specialist schools due to their needs. However, home education requires a lot of commitment from parents and may be challenging for some families.

Effective Strategies for Supporting Learning and Development

Effective strategies for supporting learning and development in individuals with ASD are those that are tailored to the individual's strengths and needs. These strategies must be evidence-based and supported by research. Some effective strategies for supporting learning and development in individuals with ASD include:

Visual Aids - Visual aids, such as pictures, diagrams, and flowcharts, can be helpful for individuals with ASD who have difficulty processing verbal information.

Positive Reinforcement - Positive reinforcement, such as praise and rewards, can be used to encourage positive behavior and promote learning.

Social Skills Training - Social skills training can help individuals with ASD to develop their social communication skills and build positive relationships with others.

Assistive Technology - Assistive technology, such as communication devices and software, can be helpful for individuals with ASD who have difficulty with communication.

Sensory Integration Therapy - Sensory integration therapy can help individuals with ASD who have sensory processing difficulties to regulate their responses to sensory input.

Education is crucial for individuals with ASD, and early intervention is key to providing effective educational support. There are several types of educational settings and programs available in the UK, including mainstream schools, specialist schools, and home education. Effective strategies for supporting learning and development in individuals with ASD include visual aids, positive reinforcement, social skills training, assistive technology, and sensory integration therapy. It is important to remember that educational support must be individualized and based on the individual's strengths and needs to promote the best possible outcomes.

<u>**Chapter 10: Employment and ASD**</u>

Autism Spectrum Disorder (ASD) is a developmental condition that affects communication, social interaction, and behavior. As individuals with ASD grow and develop, they often face challenges in finding and maintaining employment. In this chapter, we will examine the challenges faced by individuals with ASD in the workplace, highlight their unique strengths and skills, and discuss strategies for promoting employment opportunities and success.

Challenges in the Workplace

Individuals with ASD may face various challenges in the workplace, such as difficulty with communication and social interaction, sensory sensitivities, and executive function difficulties. These challenges can make it challenging to navigate the social and professional expectations of a workplace environment, leading to misunderstandings, conflicts, and other barriers to success.

Moreover, individuals with ASD may struggle to secure and maintain employment due to prejudice and discrimination. Employers may be hesitant to hire individuals with ASD due to a lack of understanding or assumptions about their capabilities. In some cases, individuals with ASD may also experience bullying or harassment in the workplace, making it challenging to feel comfortable and confident in their work environment.

Strengths and Skills

Despite the challenges that individuals with ASD may face in the workplace, they also possess unique strengths and skills that can make them valuable employees. Individuals with ASD are often highly detail-oriented and have excellent memory and analytical skills, making them well-suited for tasks that require precision and attention to detail. They may also have a strong ability to focus on a task for an extended period, which can be beneficial in roles that require sustained concentration.

Furthermore, individuals with ASD may have a unique perspective and approach to problem-solving, which can lead to creative and innovative solutions. They may also possess a high level of loyalty and dedication to their work and can be highly dependable employees.

Strategies for Promoting Employment Opportunities and Success

To promote employment opportunities and success for individuals with ASD, it is essential to address the challenges they may face and leverage their unique strengths and skills. Here are some strategies that can be useful:

Educate Employers: Employers should receive training and education about ASD and how it can impact job performance. This can help reduce misconceptions and prejudices and create a more inclusive and supportive work environment.

Provide Accommodations: Employers can provide accommodations such as modified work schedules, reduced sensory stimuli, and clear instructions and expectations to support individuals with ASD in the workplace.

Develop Social Skills: Individuals with ASD can benefit from training in social skills to help them navigate workplace expectations and communicate effectively with colleagues and supervisors.

Promote Job Coaching: Job coaching can provide individuals with ASD with support and guidance in learning new tasks and navigating workplace dynamics.

Foster Inclusivity: Employers can foster inclusivity in the workplace by promoting diversity and creating a supportive and accepting work environment.

Individuals with ASD possess unique strengths and skills that can make them valuable employees. However, they may also face challenges in the workplace due to communication and social difficulties, sensory sensitivities, and executive function difficulties. To promote employment opportunities and success for individuals with ASD, it is essential to address these challenges and leverage their unique strengths and skills. Through education, accommodation, social skills training, job coaching, and fostering inclusivity, individuals with ASD can thrive in the workplace and make significant contributions to their organizations.

<u>**Chapter 11: Relationships and Intimacy for Individuals with ASD**</u>

For individuals with Autism Spectrum Disorder (ASD), forming and maintaining relationships can be a challenge. The social and communication difficulties that are characteristic of ASD can make it difficult for individuals with ASD to understand social cues, make and maintain friendships, and engage in romantic relationships. However, with the right support, individuals with ASD can build healthy relationships and experience intimacy.

Challenges in Relationships for Individuals with ASD

The social and communication difficulties experienced by individuals with ASD can make forming relationships a challenge. Individuals with ASD may struggle to understand social cues, such as facial expressions and body language, making it difficult for them to interpret others' feelings and intentions. This can lead to misunderstandings and social isolation.

In addition, individuals with ASD may have difficulty initiating and maintaining conversations, expressing their own thoughts and feelings, and understanding social norms and rules. These difficulties can make it hard for individuals with ASD to build friendships and social connections.

When it comes to romantic relationships, individuals with ASD may have unique challenges. For example, individuals with ASD may struggle with physical touch or sensory input, which can make it difficult for them to engage in physical intimacy. They may also have difficulty with emotional regulation, making it hard for them to understand and manage their own emotions or those of their partner.

Experiences of Romantic Relationships for Individuals with ASD

Despite these challenges, individuals with ASD are capable of forming romantic relationships and experiencing intimacy. However, it is important to acknowledge and address the unique experiences that individuals with ASD may have in romantic relationships.

For example, individuals with ASD may struggle with the ambiguity and uncertainty that are often present in romantic relationships. They may prefer clear rules and guidelines, and may have difficulty navigating the unspoken rules and expectations that are often part of romantic relationships. This can lead to anxiety and confusion, and may make it hard for individuals with ASD to initiate and maintain romantic relationships.

In addition, individuals with ASD may have difficulty understanding and expressing emotions, which can make it hard for them to communicate effectively with their partner. They may also struggle with physical touch or sensory input, which can make physical intimacy challenging.

Supporting Healthy Relationships and Intimacy for Individuals with ASD

Despite these challenges, it is possible for individuals with ASD to build healthy relationships and experience intimacy. It is important to provide support that is tailored to the individual's unique needs and preferences.

One approach that can be helpful is social skills training. Social skills training can help individuals with ASD to understand social norms and rules, build communication skills, and develop strategies for initiating and maintaining relationships. This can help to reduce social isolation and increase opportunities for building friendships and romantic relationships.

In addition, it can be helpful to provide education and support around sexuality and intimacy. This can include providing information about sexual health, consent, and relationship boundaries, as well as helping individuals with ASD to develop strategies for managing physical touch and sensory input.

It is also important to support emotional regulation and communication skills. This can include helping individuals with ASD to identify and express their own emotions, as well as to understand and respond to the emotions of others. Developing these skills can help to reduce anxiety and confusion in romantic relationships, and can help to build stronger emotional connections with partners.

Chapter 12: Independent Living for Individuals with ASD

Autism Spectrum Disorder (ASD) affects an individual's social communication, behavior, and sensory processing. This condition has no known cure and typically lasts throughout the individual's life. Independent living is a goal for individuals with ASD, but it comes with unique challenges that can make it difficult to achieve. In this chapter, we will explore the challenges of independent living for individuals with ASD, effective strategies for promoting independence, and the importance of community supports.

Challenges of Independent Living for Individuals with ASD

Many individuals with ASD have difficulty with executive functioning skills such as planning, organization, and time management. This can make it challenging to maintain a routine, pay bills, and manage daily living activities. Additionally, social communication difficulties can lead to challenges with finding and keeping employment, building and maintaining relationships, and navigating social situations.

Sensory processing differences can also make independent living more challenging for individuals with ASD. For example, some individuals with ASD may experience sensory overload in noisy or crowded environments, making it difficult to shop for groceries or navigate public transportation. Others may have sensory seeking behaviors, such as spinning or flapping, that can make it challenging to live independently.

Effective Strategies for Promoting Independence

Despite the challenges, many individuals with ASD can achieve independence with the right supports and strategies. Here are some effective strategies for promoting independence:

Establishing Routines and Structure - Routines and structure can help individuals with ASD manage their time and activities more effectively. This can include daily routines, visual schedules, and reminders to help them stay on track.

Developing Self-Advocacy Skills - Teaching individuals with ASD self-advocacy skills can help them communicate their needs effectively and advocate for themselves in social situations, healthcare settings, and employment.

Identifying Strengths and Interests - Identifying an individual's strengths and interests can help them find meaningful employment and develop hobbies that promote social interaction and independence.

Teaching Life Skills - Teaching life skills such as cooking, cleaning, and budgeting can help individuals with ASD manage daily living activities more effectively.

Providing Social Skills Training - Social skills training can help individuals with ASD learn how to build and maintain relationships, navigate social situations, and communicate effectively.

Importance of Community Supports

Community supports are essential for individuals with ASD to achieve independent living. This can include support from family members, friends, and professionals such as doctors, therapists, and support workers. Additionally, community supports such as support groups, social clubs, and employment programs can provide opportunities for individuals with ASD to connect with others and develop important skills.

In the UK, there are various community supports available for individuals with ASD. For example, the National Autistic Society (NAS) provides support and services such as advice lines, support groups, and employment services. Additionally, the government provides disability benefits such as Personal Independence Payment (PIP) and Employment and Support Allowance (ESA) to support individuals with disabilities, including those with ASD.

Independent living is a goal for many individuals with ASD, but it comes with unique challenges. However, with the right supports and strategies, individuals with ASD can achieve independence and live fulfilling lives. Establishing routines and structure, developing self-advocacy skills, identifying strengths and interests, teaching life skills, and providing social skills training can all promote independence. Additionally, community supports such as family, friends, and professionals, as well as support groups, social clubs, and employment programs, can provide opportunities for individuals with ASD to connect with others and develop important skills.

<u>Chapter 13: Family Support for Individuals with ASD</u>

Autism Spectrum Disorder (ASD) not only affects the individual with the diagnosis, but it also impacts their family members. Families play a critical role in supporting individuals with ASD, and it is important to acknowledge and address their needs. In this chapter, we will examine the impact of ASD on families, highlight effective strategies for providing support, and discuss the importance of family-centered care in the UK.

Impact of ASD on Families

ASD can have a significant impact on families. The diagnosis can bring about a range of emotions, including shock, grief, denial, and anxiety. Families may also experience increased stress and financial burden due to the cost of therapy, medical appointments, and other related expenses. Additionally, the daily challenges of caring for an individual with ASD, such as communication difficulties and sensory issues, can take a toll on family members.

Siblings of individuals with ASD may also be impacted. They may feel neglected or resentful of the attention given to their sibling with ASD, or they may struggle to understand their sibling's behaviors and communication. Parents of individuals with ASD may also face difficulties in balancing the needs of their child with ASD with the needs of their other children.

Effective Strategies for Providing Support

Providing support to families of individuals with ASD is crucial for their wellbeing. One effective strategy is to provide access to information and resources. In the UK, there are many organizations and support groups that provide information and guidance for families of individuals with ASD. These organizations can offer advice on navigating the education and healthcare systems, finding appropriate therapies and interventions, and accessing financial support.

Another strategy is to provide emotional support. This can be done through counselling services, peer support groups, or respite care. Counselling services can help family members process their emotions and develop coping strategies. Peer support groups can provide a sense of community and connection with others who are going through similar experiences. Respite care can provide family members with a break from their caregiving duties and allow them to recharge.

Family-Centered Care

Family-centered care is an approach to healthcare that recognizes the importance of the family in supporting the health and wellbeing of the individual with ASD. It involves working collaboratively with families to develop individualized care plans that address the needs of the entire family.

In the UK, family-centered care is becoming increasingly recognized as an important component of ASD treatment. This approach involves listening to and respecting the preferences and values of the family, and involving them in decision-making about their loved one's care. It also involves providing education and training to families to help them develop the skills and knowledge they need to support their loved one with ASD.

ASD not only affects the individual with the diagnosis, but it also impacts their families. Providing support to families is crucial for their wellbeing, and there are many effective strategies for doing so. In the UK, family-centered care is becoming increasingly recognized as an important component of ASD treatment. By working collaboratively with families, healthcare providers can develop individualized care plans that address the needs of the entire family.

Chapter 14: Advocacy for Individuals with ASD

Autism Spectrum Disorder (ASD) is a complex condition that affects individuals in many ways. It is a lifelong condition that affects how a person thinks, feels, communicates and interacts with others. Although there is no cure for ASD, early intervention and appropriate support can help individuals with ASD to reach their full potential. Advocacy is an essential aspect of ensuring that individuals with ASD receive the support and accommodations they need to thrive. In this chapter, we will explore the importance of advocacy for individuals with ASD, effective strategies for self-advocacy, and the importance of allyship and advocacy at the community and policy levels.

Advocacy for individuals with ASD is crucial in ensuring that they have equal access to education, healthcare, employment opportunities, and other important services. Unfortunately, many individuals with ASD face barriers to accessing these services due to a lack of understanding of their needs or discrimination based on their diagnosis. Advocacy can help individuals with ASD to overcome these barriers by raising awareness of their needs, educating others about the challenges they face, and promoting policies that support their inclusion and full participation in society.

One effective strategy for self-advocacy is to develop a strong understanding of one's strengths and weaknesses. Individuals with ASD may have unique talents and abilities that can be harnessed to achieve success in various fields. Self-advocacy involves identifying these strengths and communicating them to others to showcase their value. This can be done by developing a personal brand or marketing oneself in a positive light to potential employers, educators, or healthcare providers.

Another critical aspect of self-advocacy is to communicate one's needs effectively. Individuals with ASD may have unique communication challenges, which can make it difficult to express their needs clearly. It is essential to find effective communication strategies, such as using visual aids or written communication, to ensure that others understand their needs. Practicing these skills in safe environments can help individuals with ASD to feel more confident in expressing their needs in everyday situations.

In addition to self-advocacy, it is important to have allies in the community who can advocate for the needs and rights of individuals with ASD. This can include family members, friends, educators, healthcare professionals, and community leaders. By working together, these allies can create a more inclusive and supportive environment for individuals with ASD.

At the policy level, advocacy can involve lobbying for legislative changes that benefit individuals with ASD and their families. This can include policies related to education, healthcare, employment, and community services. Advocacy groups and organizations can play a key role in this process by bringing attention to the needs and challenges faced by individuals with ASD, and by advocating for change on their behalf.

Overall, advocacy is a crucial aspect of supporting individuals with ASD and promoting a more inclusive society. By empowering individuals with ASD to self-advocate and by building strong allies and communities, we can work towards a future where individuals with ASD are fully included and have the support they need to thrive.

<u>**Chapter 15: Autism and Aging**</u>

Autism is a lifelong developmental disorder that affects individuals across the lifespan. While much attention has been given to the challenges faced by children and young adults with autism, relatively little is known about how the disorder affects individuals as they age. This is a particularly important issue given that the prevalence of autism is increasing, with the number of individuals with autism in the UK projected to reach 2.7 million by 2025.

As individuals with autism age, they may face a range of challenges that can affect their physical and mental health, as well as their ability to live independently. Some of the key challenges faced by older adults with autism include:

Health issues: Individuals with autism may be more susceptible to certain health conditions, such as epilepsy, gastrointestinal problems, and sleep disorders. These health issues can be particularly challenging for aging adults with autism, who may also be dealing with age-related health problems.

Social isolation: Individuals with autism may have difficulty forming and maintaining social relationships, which can be compounded as they age and experience changes in their living situation and support network.

Financial insecurity: Many individuals with autism struggle to find and maintain employment, which can make it difficult for them to achieve financial stability. This can be particularly challenging as they age and may need to rely on their savings or retirement income.

Lack of appropriate support: As individuals with autism age, their needs for support may change, and it can be difficult to find appropriate support services and care providers that are knowledgeable about autism and can provide the specialized support that they require.

In order to address these challenges, it is important to promote health and wellness in aging adults with autism. This can include:

Regular medical check-ups: Aging adults with autism should receive regular medical check-ups in order to identify and treat any health issues early on.

Social support: It is important for individuals with autism to have a strong social support network, which can help to reduce social isolation and promote mental health.

Financial planning: Individuals with autism and their families should work with financial planners and other professionals to develop a plan for long-term financial stability and security.

Specialized support services: Aging adults with autism may require specialized support services, such as occupational therapy or speech therapy, in order to maintain their independence and quality of life.

It is also important to raise awareness about the unique challenges faced by aging adults with autism and to advocate for policies and programs that support their needs. This can include:

Increased funding for research: More research is needed to better understand the challenges faced by aging adults with autism and to develop effective interventions and support services.

Training for healthcare professionals: Healthcare professionals should receive training on how to provide appropriate care for aging adults with autism.

Access to specialized care: Aging adults with autism should have access to specialized care providers who are knowledgeable about autism and can provide the support they need.

Advocacy for policy change: Advocacy efforts should focus on promoting policies and programs that support the needs of aging adults with autism, such as increased funding for support services and care providers.

Chapter 16: Research and Treatment for ASD

Autism Spectrum Disorder (ASD) is a complex neurodevelopmental disorder that affects communication, social interaction, and behavior. Over the years, there have been numerous research studies conducted to better understand ASD and develop effective treatments.

One of the most widely used treatments for ASD is Applied Behavior Analysis (ABA) therapy. ABA therapy is a behavior-based therapy that uses positive reinforcement to teach individuals with ASD new skills and reduce problem behaviors. While ABA therapy has been shown to be effective in improving skills such as communication, socialization, and daily living, it is not without controversy.

Critics of ABA therapy argue that the focus on behavior modification and normalization can be harmful to individuals with ASD. ABA therapy often involves breaking down complex skills into small, measurable steps and providing rewards for achieving each step. Critics argue that this approach can be dehumanizing and lead to a focus on compliance rather than empowerment.

Furthermore, there have been reports of harmful side effects associated with ABA therapy. Some individuals who have undergone ABA therapy report feeling traumatized and experiencing PTSD-like symptoms. The intensive nature of ABA therapy, which can involve up to 40 hours per week of therapy, can also lead to burnout and fatigue for both the individual with ASD and their caregivers.

It is important for individuals considering ABA therapy as a treatment option to carefully weigh the potential benefits and risks. While ABA therapy has been shown to be effective in improving skills in some individuals with ASD, it is not a one-size-fits-all approach. It is crucial to consider individual needs and preferences when selecting a treatment plan.

Furthermore, it is important for ABA therapists to prioritize the well-being and autonomy of the individuals with ASD they work with. This includes taking a person-centered approach that recognizes the individual's unique strengths, interests, and needs, and avoiding harmful practices such as punishment and aversive therapies.

In addition to ABA therapy, there are other evidence-based treatments available for individuals with ASD. These include speech therapy, occupational therapy, and social skills training. It is important to work with a qualified healthcare professional to determine the most effective treatment plan for each individual with ASD.

When it comes to research on ASD and potential treatments, it is crucial that researchers prioritize ethical considerations. This includes obtaining informed consent from study participants and ensuring that their autonomy and well-being are protected throughout the research process. It is also important to prioritize diverse representation in research studies to ensure that findings are applicable to a wide range of individuals with ASD.

while ABA therapy has been shown to be effective in improving skills in some individuals with ASD, it is not without controversy and potential harm. It is important for individuals with ASD and their caregivers to carefully consider the potential benefits and risks of different treatment options and prioritize the well-being and autonomy of the individual with ASD. Additionally, researchers must prioritize ethical considerations in their research on ASD and potential treatments.

Chapter 17: Support for Parents and Caregivers of Individuals with ASD

Caring for a child or loved one with Autism Spectrum Disorder (ASD) can be both rewarding and challenging. Parents and caregivers of individuals with ASD often face unique challenges that can impact their mental and physical well-being. It is crucial for them to have access to support and resources to help manage the demands of caregiving and maintain their own health.

One of the challenges faced by parents and caregivers of individuals with ASD is the emotional toll of constantly advocating and navigating complex healthcare and educational systems. Parents and caregivers may also experience feelings of isolation and social exclusion due to the stigma surrounding ASD. These challenges can lead to increased levels of stress, anxiety, and depression, affecting the mental health of parents and caregivers.

It is important for parents and caregivers to prioritize self-care and seek out support to mitigate the negative effects of caregiving. One strategy is to find a support group, either in person or online, for parents and caregivers of individuals with ASD. These groups can provide a safe space for sharing experiences, challenges, and successes, as well as offering emotional support and practical advice. The National Autistic Society and the Autism Alliance UK are two organizations that offer support groups for parents and caregivers.

Another important strategy is to seek out respite care, which can provide temporary relief for caregivers. Respite care can include a professional caregiver or a trusted family member or friend who can take over caregiving responsibilities for a period of time. This allows caregivers to take a break, attend to their own needs, and recharge.

Accessing community resources and services is also important for parents and caregivers of individuals with ASD. These resources can include social services, educational programs, and healthcare providers. The UK government provides funding for assessments, care planning, and support services through local authorities. The Autism Education Trust provides guidance on educational support and has a directory of resources and services for parents and caregivers.

In addition to community resources, there are also online resources available to support parents and caregivers of individuals with ASD. The National Autistic Society has an online community forum where parents and caregivers can connect with each other and find support. The Autism Helpline, run by the National Autistic Society, also provides information, advice, and support to parents and caregivers.

It is important for parents and caregivers to prioritize their own health and well-being in order to provide the best care for their loved one with ASD. This can include practicing self-care strategies such as mindfulness, exercise, and therapy. Caregivers should also be aware of the signs of burnout and seek professional help if necessary.

Parents and caregivers of individuals with ASD face unique challenges that can impact their mental and physical well-being. It is crucial for them to have access to support and resources to help manage the demands of caregiving and maintain their own health. Strategies such as finding a support group, seeking out respite care, accessing community resources and services, and practicing self-care can help mitigate the negative effects of caregiving. It is important for parents and caregivers to prioritize their own health and well-being in order to provide the best care for their loved one with ASD.

Chapter 18: Advocating for Inclusion and Acceptance of Individuals with ASD

Autism spectrum disorder (ASD) affects about 1 in every 100 people in the UK, making it a common neurodevelopmental disorder. Despite this, individuals with ASD often face social exclusion and stigmatization in society. This makes it important for individuals, communities, and society to promote inclusion and acceptance of individuals with ASD. In this chapter, we will examine the role of these stakeholders in promoting acceptance, effective strategies for reducing stigma, and the importance of diversity, equity, and inclusion for individuals with ASD.

The Role of Individuals, Communities, and Society in Promoting Inclusion and Acceptance of Individuals with ASD

Inclusive attitudes and behaviors towards individuals with ASD can be promoted by individuals, communities, and society. Individuals can foster inclusion and acceptance of individuals with ASD by learning about the condition and challenging stereotypes and misconceptions about ASD. Communities can create inclusive environments that accommodate individuals with ASD, for example, by offering sensory-friendly events or creating inclusive workplaces. Society can promote inclusion and acceptance of individuals with ASD by creating laws and policies that protect their rights and ensure access to education, healthcare, and other services.

Effective Strategies for Reducing Stigma

Stigma and discrimination towards individuals with ASD can lead to social exclusion, which can negatively impact their mental health, self-esteem, and quality of life. Effective strategies for reducing stigma towards individuals with ASD include increasing awareness and education about ASD, challenging stereotypes and misconceptions about the condition, promoting positive portrayals of individuals with ASD in media and entertainment, and offering support and resources for individuals with ASD and their families. It is also important to involve individuals with ASD in initiatives that aim to reduce stigma towards them, as they can provide valuable insights into their experiences and needs.

The Importance of Diversity, Equity, and Inclusion for Individuals with ASD

Promoting diversity, equity, and inclusion for individuals with ASD is essential for their wellbeing and development. Diversity refers to the recognition and acceptance of differences in individuals with ASD, such as different communication styles or sensory needs. Equity refers to ensuring that individuals with ASD have access to the same opportunities and resources as others, for example, access to education and healthcare. Inclusion refers to creating an environment where individuals with ASD feel welcomed, valued, and able to participate fully in society.

The benefits of promoting diversity, equity, and inclusion for individuals with ASD are numerous. For example, individuals with ASD who are included in education and employment settings are more likely to achieve their full potential, have higher self-esteem, and experience better mental health outcomes. Inclusive environments also benefit society by promoting diversity, reducing discrimination and stigma, and contributing to a more equitable and just society.

Promoting inclusion and acceptance of individuals with ASD is essential for their wellbeing and development. Individuals, communities, and society all play a role in promoting inclusion and reducing stigma towards individuals with ASD. Effective strategies for reducing stigma include increasing awareness and education about ASD, promoting positive portrayals of individuals with ASD in media and entertainment, and offering support and resources for individuals with ASD and their families. Promoting diversity, equity, and inclusion for individuals with ASD benefits not only individuals with ASD but also society as a whole by promoting diversity, reducing discrimination and stigma, and contributing to a more equitable and just society.

Chapter 19: Living with ASD: Personal Perspectives

Autism Spectrum Disorder (ASD) is a developmental disorder that affects an estimated 1 in 100 people in the UK. Despite its prevalence, the condition is often misunderstood, and people with ASD can face numerous challenges in their daily lives. In this chapter, we will hear from individuals with ASD and their families, sharing their personal experiences and perspectives.

ASD is a complex condition that affects individuals in different ways. Some people with ASD have difficulty with social interactions and communication, while others may struggle with sensory processing or have obsessive interests. For many individuals, these differences can make it challenging to navigate the world around them and connect with others.

One individual, Emily, was diagnosed with ASD when she was in her late teens. She described her experiences as feeling like she was "from a different planet," struggling to understand the social cues and expectations of those around her. Emily found it difficult to make friends, and her family often struggled to understand her behavior. However, after her diagnosis, Emily was able to access the support she needed to manage her condition and develop strategies to navigate social situations more effectively.

Another individual, Sam, has a young son with ASD. Sam described the challenges of navigating the education system and accessing appropriate support for her son. She also spoke of the social isolation that many families of individuals with ASD experience, as others may not understand the condition and the impact it can have on daily life. However, Sam remains optimistic and believes that with the right support, her son can thrive and live a fulfilling life.

For many individuals with ASD, the condition can present significant challenges in daily life. However, it is important to recognise that everyone with ASD is different, and there is no "one size fits all" approach to supporting individuals with the condition.

One aspect of living with ASD that is often overlooked is the strengths and talents that individuals with the condition can bring. Many people with ASD have a unique perspective on the world and possess skills and interests that can be valuable to society. For example, some individuals with ASD excel in science, technology, engineering, and maths (STEM) fields, while others may have a particular talent for art or music.

It is crucial that society recognises and values the contributions of individuals with ASD, and that opportunities are provided to help them thrive. This can include creating inclusive workplaces that recognise the strengths of individuals with ASD, and providing support for individuals to develop their interests and skills.

Another important aspect of living with ASD is the need for understanding and acceptance from society. People with ASD may face stigma and discrimination due to their condition, which can have a significant impact on their mental health and wellbeing. It is crucial that society works to reduce the stigma surrounding ASD and promotes acceptance of individuals with the condition.

This can include educating people about ASD and raising awareness of the challenges faced by those with the condition. It can also involve creating opportunities for individuals with ASD to participate in society and reducing barriers to inclusion.

Chapter 20: The Future of ASD

Autism spectrum disorder (ASD) affects millions of individuals worldwide, and its prevalence continues to rise. In the UK alone, an estimated 700,000 individuals are on the autism spectrum. While much progress has been made in understanding and supporting individuals with ASD, there is still much work to be done. In this chapter, we will examine the current trends and future directions in ASD research, treatment, and support, highlighting the potential for advancements in understanding and supporting individuals with ASD. We will also discuss the importance of continued advocacy, research, and collaboration in improving outcomes for individuals with ASD.

Research on ASD has been expanding rapidly in recent years. In the past decade, there has been a significant increase in the number of studies investigating the genetic and environmental factors contributing to ASD. Advancements in neuroimaging techniques have also allowed for a better understanding of the brain mechanisms involved in ASD. Researchers are now exploring the potential of early intervention and prevention strategies, with the aim of improving outcomes for individuals with ASD.

Another promising area of research is the development of personalized treatments. While there is no cure for ASD, evidence-based interventions have been shown to improve outcomes for individuals with ASD. However, not all individuals with ASD respond to the same interventions. Personalized treatments that take into account an individual's specific needs and strengths may be more effective than a one-size-fits-all approach. This personalized approach may involve the use of technology, such as virtual reality, to provide tailored interventions.

Advancements in technology are also providing new opportunities for individuals with ASD. Augmentative and alternative communication (AAC) devices have been shown to improve communication skills in individuals with ASD. Virtual reality and gaming technologies are also being developed to improve social skills and reduce anxiety in individuals with ASD. These technologies have the potential to provide new and innovative ways of supporting individuals with ASD.

In terms of support for individuals with ASD, there has been a shift towards a more person-centered approach. This approach involves taking into account an individual's unique needs, strengths, and preferences, and providing support that is tailored to their specific requirements. This approach recognizes that individuals with ASD have diverse experiences and challenges, and that support should be flexible and adaptable.

There has also been a growing recognition of the importance of community-based support. Community support programs can provide valuable opportunities for social interaction and skill development for individuals with ASD. These programs can also provide support and respite for caregivers, who often face significant challenges in caring for individuals with ASD.

Despite these advancements, there are still many challenges faced by individuals with ASD and their families. Stigma and discrimination remain significant barriers to inclusion and acceptance for individuals with ASD. The lack of understanding and awareness of ASD can also contribute to difficulties in accessing appropriate support and services. There is a need for continued advocacy, education, and awareness-raising to promote inclusion and acceptance of individuals with ASD.

In conclusion, there is much potential for advancements in understanding and supporting individuals with ASD. Research on genetic and environmental factors, personalized treatments, and innovative technologies are providing new opportunities for improving outcomes for individuals with ASD. A person-centered approach and community-based support are also important in providing tailored support and opportunities for social interaction and skill development. However, there is still much work to be done in promoting inclusion and reducing stigma and discrimination for individuals with ASD. Continued advocacy, education, and collaboration are essential in improving outcomes for individuals with ASD and their families.

END

Thank you for taking the time to read this Introduction to a Neurodiverse World book.

We have a range of books within this series that are steadily being released.

Topics Covered include
- Autism
- ADHD
- Sensory Processing Disorder (SPD)
- Pathological Demand Avoidance (PDA)
- Avoidant Restrictive Food Intake Disorder (ARFID)

We also post weekly articles on our website and our social media sites (links Below)

Divergent Consultants are accredited Counsellors and Psychotherapists who specialise in Spectrum Disorders.

Started by Gareth Croot when his 3 year old Non-Verbal son was diagnosed with Autism Spectrum Disorder, Global Development Delay and Hypermobility.

This lead his family on a journey resulting in his 12 year old daughter starting the ASD diagnostic pathway and Gareth also being diagnosed with Autism, PDA, Hypermobility and awaiting ADHD assessment.

Divergent Consultants offer introduction to Autism Courses, Sleep Therapy Courses, Pre and Post diagnosis counselling for parents and newly diagnosed adults aswell as general support functions

you can visit us at www.divergentconsultants.co.uk

Facebook https://www.facebook.com/people/Divergent-Consultants/100088643106730/

TikTok https://www.tiktok.com/divergentconsultants

Instagram https://www.instagram.com/divergent_consultants/